Hello Kitty®
Craft Sticks
Activity Book

by **Mary Walsh-Kezele**

Scholastic Inc.

New York Toronto London Auckland Sydney
Mexico City New Delhi Hong Kong Buenos Aires

Thanks to Creativity for Kids (A Faber-Castell Company)
for our author, Mary Walsh-Kezele.

Illustrations by Yancey C. Labat

ISBN 0-439-32839-X

12 11 10 9 8 7 6 5 4 3 2 1   1 2 3 4 5 6/0

Printed in the U.S.A.
First Scholastic printing, January 2002

Table of Contents

Hello Kitty
Craft Sticks Party

Hello Kitty has invited her pal Tippy over for a crafts party. Just like you, Hello Kitty loves to spend time with her friends, making special projects together. Craft sticks are especially fun to work with— whether you're coloring, creating, or decorating with them!

Hello Kitty and Tippy have put together their favorite craft sticks projects for you. While you do the activities in this book, you can use your imagination to dream up your own Hello Kitty crafts, too. But whatever you do, be sure to have fun!

Let's Get Started

Along with this fun Hello Kitty activity book, you have a colorful bunch of craft sticks—large, medium, and mini. You also have super-fun sparkling rhinestones and some googly eyes. To make your projects extra-special, you also have a set of 12 Hello Kitty mini-markers. You can use these markers to decorate your craft sticks projects, draw Hello Kitty pictures, or write little notes to your special friends.

Before you begin, lay out all of the materials you'll need to make a project. Throughout the book, it's mentioned how many craft sticks to use on each craft. However, on some crafts, the number of sticks you'll be using will depend on the size of the additional material you're using (like a shoe box or a journal). When you need more craft sticks, you can buy them at your local craft or hobby store. Or you can always eat lots and lots of Popsicles and save the sticks!

To complete these crafts, you'll need some materials that you have around the house. Invite your friends to join you on a creative scavenger hunt to round them up.

Here's the list to get you started:

- **Small shoe box**
- **Small gift boxes**
- **Yarn or ribbon**
- **Cardboard**
- **Paper bags**
- **Drawing or tracing paper**

- **Toilet tissue tube**
- **Rubber bands**
- **String**
- **Scissors**
- **Tape**
- **Pencil**
- **Glue**

In the back of this book, you'll find patterns of Hello Kitty and her friends. You can trace your favorite Hello Kitty characters from these patterns, or you can use them as inspiration for your own drawings.

Hello Kitty likes to keep her work area neat and clean. Before you begin, you might want to put on an old shirt and cover your workspace with newspapers. When you're finished, don't forget to tidy up!

Pretty Hello Kitty Keepers

Beautiful Birthday Boxes:

Tippy is invited to Hello Kitty's birthday party! Let's help him make a special box for her present. Hello Kitty's birthday is on November 1. When is yours?

What You Do:

1. Glue your sticks onto the lid and sides of your box. Leave a little space (about 1 inch) at the top of the box so that you can still fit the lid on. Let the sticks dry.

2. With your markers, decorate the outside of the box with some fun party doodles and designs.

3. Create a matching gift tag with your markers and a small piece of paper. Write a special note on it for your friend. Tie the tag to the box with a piece of ribbon or yarn.

What You Need:

- Small box with a lid (cardboard jewelry boxes are the perfect size)
- Glue
- Mini craft sticks (any color)
- Marker set
- Paper
- Ribbon or yarn

Hello Kitty Says:

Make a bunch of beautiful boxes! Find a few colorful cardboard boxes. Decorate the lids with a rainbow array of craft sticks. Top off the boxes with some fabric flowers, feathers, pom-poms, pipe cleaner butterflies—anything you can dream up!

Hello Kitty's Special Little Jewelry Box:

Hello Kitty loves shopping for accessories—especially bows! You can store all of your favorite small things in this special little jewelry box.

What You Do:

1. Trace the box pattern from page 40 onto a piece of white paper. Transfer this pattern onto a piece of thin cardboard, and cut it out. (Heavy paper will also work.)

2. Use your markers to draw Hello Kitty or one of her pals on the top of the box.

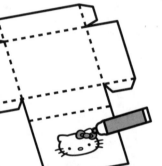

3. Fold and glue the box, as shown.

4. Cut a piece of yarn or ribbon into two 6-inch sections. Glue one piece under the edge of the top lid and the other piece to the front of the box, as shown. Let the box dry completely.

5. Now you're ready to attach the mini craft sticks. Glue four sticks (glue side down) to the top of your box to create a frame for your drawing.

6. Glue the 16 remaining sticks to the four sides of your box (four on each side) until the box is covered.

Hint: Be sure to line up the ends of the sticks to keep them even. That way, no cardboard is showing.

7. When you're finished, tie the box closed, and then decorate it with your Hello Kitty markers. Need a few design ideas? Take a peek at the patterns on pages 42–43.

What You Need:

- **Tracing paper**
- **Pencil**
- **Thin cardboard or heavy paper**
- **Scissors**
- **Marker set**
  - **Glue**
  - **Ribbon or yarn**
- **20 mini craft sticks (any color)**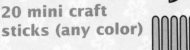

Hello Kitty Says:
Now you have a special place to store all of your favorite accessories!

Fantastic Hello Kitty Basket:

It looks like Hello Kitty and Tippy are getting ready for a picnic. You can make a special basket to hold all of your yummy treats, too.

What You Do:

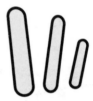

1. Start with a box, like a shoe box. Select the craft sticks size (large, medium, or mini) that best fits your box. Or use a combination of both sizes.

2. Starting on the long sides of your box, glue the craft sticks to the outside of your box horizontally (which means across). For the short sides of the box, glue your sticks on vertically (which means up and down). Let the sticks dry.

Hint: If your box is too tall, you can trim the top of it with your scissors.

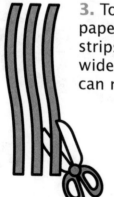

3. To make the braided basket handle, cut a paper grocery bag into three even strips. These strips should be about 24 inches long and 1 inch wide. (Depending on the size of your box, you can make these longer or shorter as needed.)

4. Tape one end of the strips together to hold them in place, then weave the strips, making a long braid.

5. Using your tape, attach both ends of the braid to the inside of your basket. If the braid is too long, trim it with your scissors.

6. Use your markers to decorate your basket.

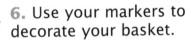

What You Need:

- One box (a child-size shoe box is just right)
- Craft sticks
- Glue
- Scissors
- Paper grocery bag
- Tape
- Marker set

Hello Kitty Says:
A tisket, a tasket, I love my picnic basket! Pack a few snacks, find a cozy spot, grab a few friends, and have a positively perfect picnic.

Hello Kitty's Perfect Pencil Pot:

You can make a perfect Hello Kitty container to hold your markers, crayons, pens, and pencils.

What You Do:

1. Start with an empty cardboard toilet tissue tube. Using your tube as a pattern, draw a circle onto a piece of cardboard. Cut out around the circle, leaving a half-inch border.

2. Center the tube on the cardboard circle, and glue it in place. Let it dry.

3. Wrap a rubber band around the middle of the tube.

4. Place a small amount of glue on one side of one of your craft sticks. Slide the stick under the rubber band so that the glue side is against the tissue tube. (The rubber band will help hold the sticks in place while the glue dries.)

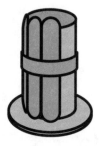

Hello Kitty Says:

I'm going to make a pencil pot for Tippy! Who will you make one for?

5. Continue gluing sticks to the tube until the tube is entirely covered, and let it dry. Remove the rubber band.

6. Use your markers to decorate the outside of your pencil pot. For extra sparkle, glue on a few rhinestones.

7. To finish your project, tie a colorful piece of yarn or ribbon around your pencil pot.

What You Need:

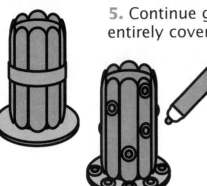

- **Cardboard toilet tissue tube**
- **Cardboard**
  - **Pencil**
  - **Scissors**
  - **Glue**
- **Rubber band**
- **Medium craft sticks**
- **Marker set**
- **Rhinestones**
- **Yarn or ribbon**

Creative Hello Kitty

Book Buddies:

Hello Kitty loves to curl up with a favorite book. You can make a Hello Kitty book buddy to read along with you.

What You Do:

1. Select your favorite Hello Kitty character from the patterns on pages 42–43. Trace two identical patterns onto your piece of paper.

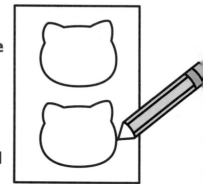

2. Decorate the faces with your markers, then cut them out. If you like, you can add a bow, rhinestones, or some fun googly eyes.

3. Glue one face shape to the top of the front of one of your craft sticks. Glue the other face to the top of the back of the stick. Adjust the paper until the faces match. If needed, add a little glue to seal the edges.

4. To make your book buddy super fancy, decorate the stick with your markers, or glue on rhinestones or googly eyes.

5. When the glue is dry, tuck the stick part of your buddy inside the pages of your favorite book to keep your place.

What You Need:

- Tracing paper
- Pencil
- Marker set
- Scissors
- Rhinestones or googly eyes (optional)
- Glue
- Large craft sticks (one per book buddy)

Hello Kitty Says:

Who's hiding inside the pages of my book?

Hello Kitty Puppet Pals:

With her cute little whiskers and her tiny pink bow, who is the star of this puppet show? Hello Kitty, of course!

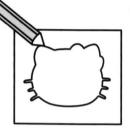

What You Do:

To Make Your Puppets:

1. Trace one of the patterns on pages 42–43 onto your construction paper, and cut it out. Use your markers to draw Hello Kitty's eyes and nose.

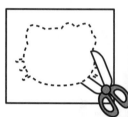

2. You can draw Hello Kitty's whiskers and hair bow using your markers, or cut them out from your construction paper and glue them onto her face. When you're finished, glue the puppet face to the top of a craft stick.

3. Hello Kitty loves to dress up Design a special outfit for her wear by tracing one of the patter on page 43 or by creating your ow Cut out and color your creation then glue it onto your stick. You can add a few rhinestones for extra sparkle.

4. Use the other patterns on pages 42–43 to make Tippy, Fifi, Kathy, and Mimmy puppets, too.

Make Your Puppet Stage:

1. Cut an opening in the bottom of the shoe box. You can make the opening fancy with extra construction paper cut out shapes so that it looks like a real stage, as shown. (You may want to ask an adult or an older friend to help you.) Flip the box over so the bottom is facing forward—this is the stage. Decorate the stage with construction paper and markers, and you're ready to begin!

2. Take your puppet pals, and hold them behind the stage. Get together with your friends, and put on your own Hello Kitty puppet pal play!

What You Need:

- **Several sheets of construction paper (any color)**
- **Tracing paper**
  - **Pencil**
  - **Scissors**
  - **Marker set**
- **Glue**
- **Large plain craft sticks (one per puppet)**
- **Rhinestones**
- **Large shoe box**

Hello Kitty Says:

Encore! Encore! Come on, Tippy, let's change costumes and get ready for the next show.

Hello Kitty Masquerade:

You can make fun Hello Kitty and Tippy masks for a masquerade party!

What You Do:

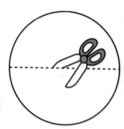

1. Draw a line down the center of a paper plate, using a pencil and a ruler. Cut along the line, dividing your plate into two sections. Keep one for your Hello Kitty mask, and set the other aside for later.

2. Turn your plate over so that the bottom is facing you, and draw two circles for eyes. Carefully cut these circles out. (You may want to ask an adult or an older friend to help you with this part.)

3. Trace around the eyeholes with your black marker. Then use your yellow marker to make a cute little Hello Kitty nose.

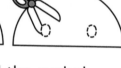

4. Cut three pairs of whiskers out of black construction paper. If you don't have black paper, you can use white paper and color it with your black marker. Glue the whiskers to the sides of the mask.

5. Cut Hello Kitty's triangle ears out of white paper, and glue them to the top of her head.

6. Now make Hello Kitty's bow. Trace the pattern on page 41 onto your favorite color paper, or draw the bow on your own. Cut it out, and glue it over Hello Kitty's left ear.

7. To make the handle of your mask, glue the end of a large craft stick to the center of the mask's underside.

8. Use the other half of the plate (which you set aside in Step 1) to make one of Hello Kitty's friends, like Kathy, Tippy, or Mimmy, Hello Kitty's twin sister. Make as many masks as you like.

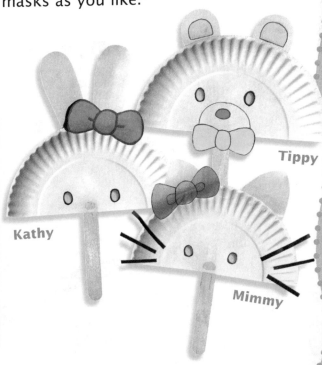

Kathy

Tippy

Mimmy

What You Need:

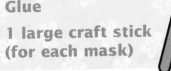

- **Paper plates (one for two masks)**
- **Pencil**
- **Ruler**
- **Scissors**
- **Marker set**
- **Construction paper (black, white, and one other color)**
- **Glue**
- **1 large craft stick (for each mask)**

Hello Kitty Dancing Streamers:

Dance, prance, pirouette. Hello Kitty loves to move to the beat of the music! You can make some streamers and dance with Hello Kitty.

What You Do:

1. Use your markers to decorate your craft sticks any way you like.

2. To make the strips, cut the crepe paper or ribbon. You can make the strips as long as your arm or even longer.

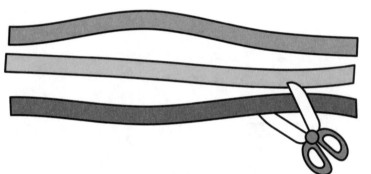

3. Attach three strips to the end of each craft stick, using tape or glue.

4. Repeat these steps to make a streamer for each of your friends. When you're finished, turn on the music, and get ready to move!

What You Need:

- **Medium or large craft sticks (any color, one per streamer)**
- **Marker set**
- **Scissors**
- **Crepe paper or ribbon (3 to 4 strips per streamer)**
- **Tape or glue**

Artistic Hello Kitty

Creative Critters:

What is flying around Hello Kitty's garden? Cute creative critters! With googly eyes, rhinestones, and a bit of glue, you can make butterflies, bees, ladybugs, and a dragonfly, too!

What You Do:

To Make a Dragonfly:

1. Select a craft stick. You can pick a colored stick or decorate a plain one with your markers.

2. Attach two googly eyes to one end of your stick and glue on some rhinestones to the rest of the stick.

3. Cut four wings out of your paper—two medium size and two small. Glue the wings to the back of your stick. First add the medium pair of wings behind the eyes, then add the small pair below it.

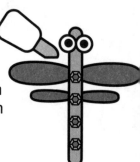

To Make a Bee:

1. Select a yellow craft stick or color a plain one. Use your black marker to add stripes to your stick.

2. Glue a pair of googly eyes to one end of the stick, then cut two small ovals out of white paper to create the wings. Use your black marker to draw a wing pattern on each.

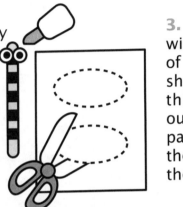

3. Glue the wings to the top of your stick, as shown. Cut two thin antennae out of black paper, and glue them to the stick, right behind the eyes. Bee-utiful!

What You Need:

- **Craft sticks (any size and color, one per bug)**
- **Marker set**
- **Googly eyes**
- **Glue**
- **Rhinestones**
- **Paper**
- **Scissors**

To Make a Butterfly:

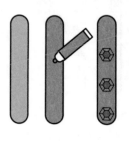

1. Select a large craft stick—this will be the body of your butterfly. Decorate your stick with markers and rhinestones. (If you want to make a mini-butterfly, use a smaller craft stick.)

2. To add the antennae, fold a twistie tie in half and glue the antennae to the back of one end of your stick. Then, glue on two googly eyes to the front of the same end of your craft stick.

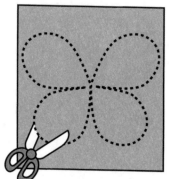

3. To make the wings, cut a piece of paper about 6 inches long by 6 inches wide, as shown here. (You can use tissue paper or construction paper.) If you're using regular paper, you can decorate the wings with your marker set.

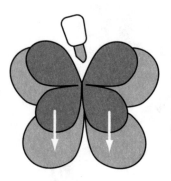

4. Make a second, smaller set of wings out of paper in a second color. Place this set of wings on top of the larger pair and glue them together. Now glue the double wings to the underside of the middle of your craft stick.

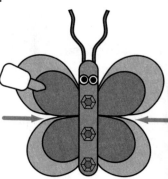

To Make a Ladybug:

1. Select a red craft stick or color a plain one. Add spots to the body with your black marker.

2. To make wings for your ladybug, cut a circle of red paper—or color your circle with red marker. Cut the circle in half, and add two black dots on each side.

3. Glue the wings to your craft stick, as shown. Add a pair of googly eyes, and your creative critter is complete.

What You Need:

- Craft sticks (any size and color, one per bug)
- Marker set
- Rhinestones
- Twistie tie
- Glue
- Googly eyes
- Scissors
- Paper (regular, construction, or tissue paper)

Hello Kitty Says:

If you're making a funky bug, you can create whatever pattern or style you like!

Hello Kitty Bitty Art:

Frame your own mini-masterpiece in an itty-bitty frame.

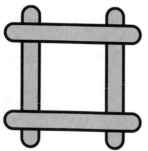

What You Do:

1. Select four mini craft sticks, and arrange them into a square, overlapping the ends slightly.

2. Glue the ends of the sticks together to hold them in place. If you want to make your picture frame decorative, add a few sparkly rhinestones.

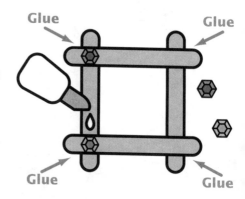

Glue

Glue

Glue

Glue

3. Cut your drawing paper to fit your frame. Then draw your mini-masterpiece with your markers. You can use the Hello Kitty patterns in the back of the book, or draw your own.

4. Center your drawing inside your frame, then tape or glue the edges to the back of the frame to hold it in place.

5. To hang your picture, glue a piece of yarn to the top back of the frame. You can even attach a magnet and hang your picture on your refrigerator or locker. Voilà! A mini-masterpiece!

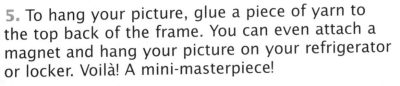

What You Need:

- 4 mini craft sticks
- Tape or glue
- Rhinestones
- Scissors
- Drawing paper
- Marker set
- Yarn

Easy Easel:

With her new easel, Hello Kitty and Tippy can make beautiful paintings together!

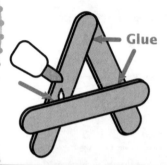
Glue

What You Do:

1. Select three large craft sticks, and arrange them into a letter A shape. Glue the sticks together to hold them in place.

2. Apply glue along one edge of your fourth stick. Place this stick across the bottom of the center stick, as shown. You may need to hold it in place until the glue sets a little. Let it dry.

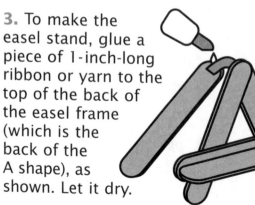
Glue

3. To make the easel stand, glue a piece of 1-inch-long ribbon or yarn to the top of the back of the easel frame (which is the back of the A shape), as shown. Let it dry.

Hello Kitty Says:

Have you made more mini-masterpieces (pages 24–25) than you can display on your easel?

Why not connect a couple of pictures and hang them together on your wall? All you do is tie one end of a little piece of ribbon or yarn to the bottom of one of your frames, then tie the other end to the top of another frame. Continue connecting as many mini-masterpieces as you like. When you're done, tie or glue another piece of ribbon or yarn to the top of your first frame to hang.

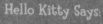

4. To finish the easel, cut another section of yarn or ribbon about 4 inches long. Glue one end of the ribbon to the center of the back of the easel frame, as shown. Glue the other end to the center back of the fifth craft stick, also as shown.

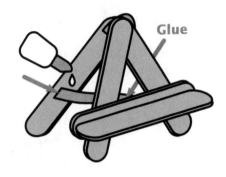

5. When your easel is dry, stand it up, and display your favorite Hello Kitty masterpiece!

What You Need:

- **5 large craft sticks**
- **Glue**
- **Ribbon or yarn**
- **Scissors**

Friendship Flowers:

Tippy loves to give Hello Kitty flowers. You can make a whole bouquet of friendship flowers to give to your friends, too!

What You Do:

1. Draw a daisy on a piece of colored construction paper. The flower should be about 3 to 4 inches wide. Cut out the flower, and set it aside.

2. On one photo of your friend, trace around your friend's face with your jar lid, so you get a nice round picture. This will be the center of your flower. Cut out the photo circle.

3. Place the circle-shaped photos in the middle of your flower, and glue it in place.

4. Glue the flower to the top of one of your craft sticks. Cut a few leaves out of the green construction paper, and glue them to your stick's stem.

5. Repeat steps 1 through 4 to make a whole bouquet!

What You Need:

- **Pencil**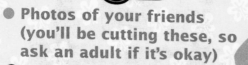
- **Colored construction paper (green and one other color)**
- **Scissors**
- **Photos of your friends (you'll be cutting these, so ask an adult if it's okay)**
  - **A small round object, like the lid of a jar**
  - **Glue**
- **Medium craft sticks (one green stick per flower)**

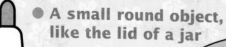

She's a Star:

Make a special wish on this Hello Kitty star.

What You Do:

1. Lay out your craft sticks in the star-shaped pattern on page 41, or as shown here.

2. Glue the ends of the sticks in place.

3. When the glue has dried, you can decorate your star with your markers, rhinestones, or sparkly glitter.

4. Make a loop of yarn or string, glue it to the top of your star, and hang it in your room.

What You Need:

- **5 medium craft sticks for each star (any color)**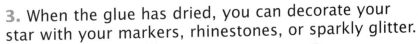
  - **Glue**
  - **Marker set**
  - **Rhinestones**
- **Glitter (optional)**
- **Yarn or string**

Hello Kitty Says:

Before you go to sleep, make a wish on your star. Sweet dreams!

Sunny Days Sun Catcher:

**Clouds and rain, go away! Hello Kitty wants to play.
Let's make a sun catcher for Hello Kitty's window.**

What You Do:

1. Arrange your craft sticks into a fun design. You can
make a diamond, square, triangle, octagon, rectangle,
or any other shape you like. Then glue the sticks together.

2. Take a piece of wax paper, and fold it in
half. Trim the edges so that it's the same size and shape
as your
craft stick
shape, and
set aside.

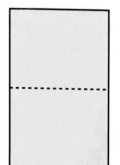

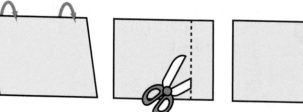

3. Cut some fun Hello Kitty designs out of
your tissue paper, using the patterns on
pages 42–43, or create your own. Unfold
your piece of wax paper and arrange the
tissue shapes on one half of it.

4. In a cup, mix a small amount of
glue with a few drops of water. Paint this
solution over your tissue shapes to hold them
in place.

5. When you're finished gluing your design in place, again fold your sheet of wax paper in half, lining up the edges. Paint the solution of glue and water over your folded sheet of wax paper to seal both halves together. Let it dry.

6. Squeeze some glue along the edges of your craft stick shape. This will be the back of your sun catcher. Then set the wax paper design in place. Let it dry.

7. Glue a loop of yarn or string to the back of your sun catcher. When the glue is dry, hang it front-side forward in a sunny window.

What You Need:

- **3 to 8 medium craft sticks (any color)**
- **Glue**
- **Wax paper**
- **Scissors**
- **Tissue paper**
- **Small cup of water**
- **Paintbrush**
- **Yarn or string**

Hello Kitty Says:

Hang the sun catcher in your room to add bright colors to your day!

Cool Cat's Eye:

You can use the yarn to weave a beautiful cat's eye design. It's so much fun to do!

What You Do:

1. Arrange two craft sticks into the cross shape shown, then glue them together.

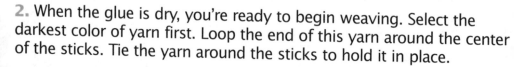

2. When the glue is dry, you're ready to begin weaving. Select the darkest color of yarn first. Loop the end of this yarn around the center of the sticks. Tie the yarn around the sticks to hold it in place.

3. Wrap the yarn around the center three or four times one way to secure the yarn to the craft sticks.

4. Change directions, wrapping the yarn the other way. Continue working until the middle of your cross is covered.

5. Take the end of the yarn, and begin weaving under and over each of the four sides of your cross shape. As you weave, turn the shape in a circle, and pull the yarn firmly.

Hello Kitty Says:

Hey Tippy, I made this cat's eye just for you!

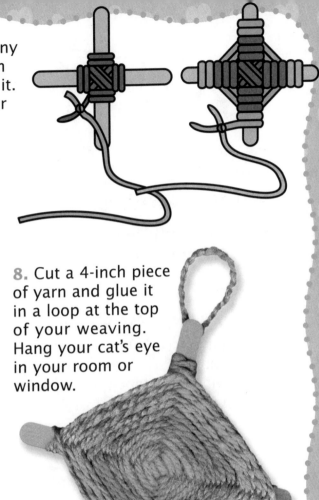

6. You can switch colors of yarn at any time. Simply cut the end of your yarn and tie on a new color to the end of it. (Using different colors will make your cat's-eye design more interesting.)

7. Stop weaving when you reach the ends of the four sides of your cross. Cut the yarn, leaving about an inch extra, and tie it around the craft stick to secure it in place. To keep the yarn from falling off, be sure to leave a little stick showing.

8. Cut a 4-inch piece of yarn and glue it in a loop at the top of your weaving. Hang your cat's eye in your room or window.

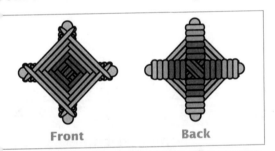

Front   Back

What You Need:

- **2 medium craft sticks (in the same color)**
- **Glue**
- **3 or 4 colors of yarn**
- **Scissors**

Exciting Writing
with Hello Kitty

Secret Messages:

Hello Kitty and Tippy send each other top-secret messages. Now you and your friends can, too!

What You Do:

Secret Message Mix-Up:

1. Write a message to a friend on your mini or medium craft sticks, using a marker. Write a single sentence or just a few words on each stick.

| my birthday |
| invited to |
| you are |
| please come! |

2. When your message is complete, put the sticks into your envelope, and send them to a friend. See if your friend can arrange the sticks and figure out your secret message!

Secret Picture Puzzle:

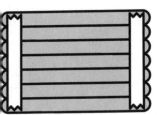

1. To send a secret picture, lay out your sticks so that they're touching. Tape the ends of the sticks together to hold them in place while you draw.

2. Draw your favorite Hello Kitty picture on the reverse side of the sticks. When you're finished, remove the tape, pop the mixed-up sticks into an envelope, and give it or send it to a friend. Hello Kitty, can you help us solve this picture puzzle?

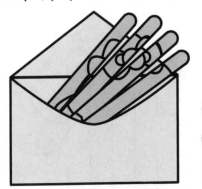

What You Need:

- **Mini or medium craft sticks**
- **Marker set**
- **Envelopes**
- **Tape**

Hello Kitty Diary:

Hidden inside where no one can see, it's Hello Kitty's diary. Hey, Tippy—no peeking!

What You Do:

1. To make the ties for your note-book, cut your ribbon into two 6-inch-long pieces. Glue one piece of ribbon to the front center of your notebook and one to the back center, as shown. The ribbons should be glued to the center edge of your book, overlapping the side that opens.

2. Select the craft sticks that best fit the size of your book. Glue them side by side to the front and back of your book until both sides are covered. You'll be gluing a stick over the edge of the ribbon in front and back of the book.

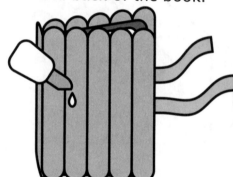

3. So that the glue holds the sticks firmly to the notebook, weigh your book down while the glue dries. To do this, place a piece of wax paper or plastic wrap over your book, then place a heavier book on top.

4. When your notebook has dried, you can decorate the cover with your markers. Or you can use one of the Hello Kitty patterns on pages 42–43, color it, and glue it to the front of your diary.

You can keep this special notebook for yourself, or you can wrap it up and give it to a special friend.

What You Need:

- Scissors
- Ribbon
- Glue
- Small notebook or notepad
- Craft sticks (size depends on how big your book is)
- Wax paper or plastic wrap
- Heavy book
- Marker set

Hello Kitty Says:

Doodle, dream, or do whatever you like inside your diary. Don't worry, your thoughts are safe with me!

Pretty Paper Scroll:

What's written on this pretty paper scroll? It's a special message fom Tippy to Hello Kitty.

What You Do:

1. Cut a piece of paper as long as you like, but narrower than the length of your craft sticks.

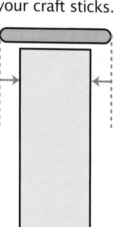

2. Use your markers to write a message on the paper, leaving some open space at the top and bottom.

Dear Hello Kitty,
Do you like t
paper

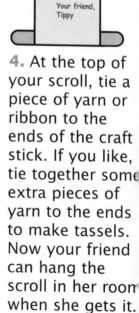

Dear Hello Kitty,

Do you like this

paper scroll?

You can write

a message or a

birthday

invitation.

Your friend,
Tippy

3. When you're finished, place a craft stick under the top and bottom of your paper. Fold the edges of the paper down over the sticks, and glue them in place.

Dear Hello Kitty,

Do you like this

paper scroll?

You can write

a message or a

birthday

invitation.

Your friend,
Tippy

4. At the top of your scroll, tie a piece of yarn or ribbon to the ends of the craft stick. If you like, tie together some extra pieces of yarn to the ends to make tassels. Now your friend can hang the scroll in her room when she gets it.

5. When the glue is dry, carefully roll the scroll up. Tie a piece of ribbon or yarn around the middle to hold the scroll closed. Now deliver it to a special friend!

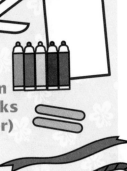

Dear Hello Kitty,

Do you like this paper Scroll?

You can write a message or a birthday invitation.

Your Friend,

Tippy

What You Need:

- **Paper**
- **Scissors**
- **Marker set**
- **2 medium craft sticks (any color)**
- **Glue**
- **Yarn or ribbon**

Hello Kitty Says:

I'm going to turn my pretty paper scrolls into party invitations.

Hello Kitty Shapes to Trace

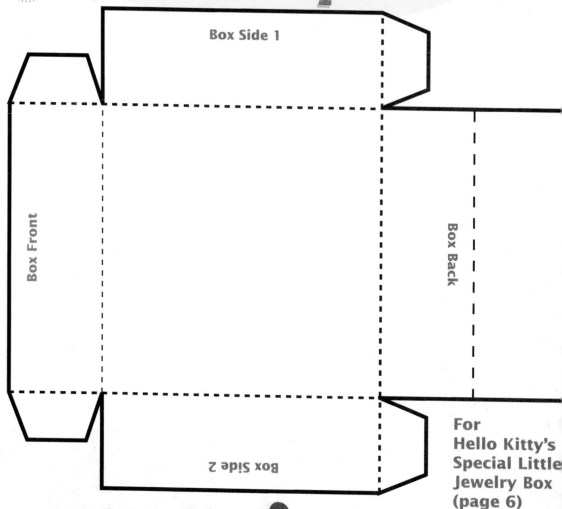

Box Side 1

Box Front

Box Back

Box Side 2

For
Hello Kitty's
Special Little
Jewelry Box
(page 6)

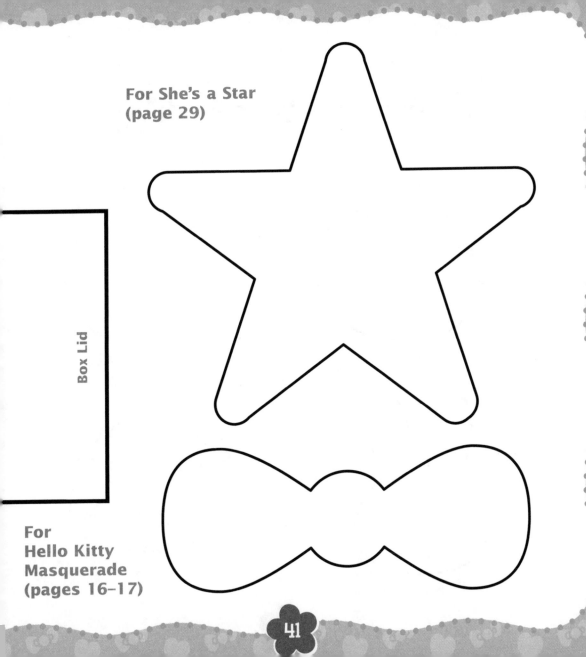

For She's a Star
(page 29)

Box Lid

**For
Hello Kitty
Masquerade
(pages 16–17)**

More Shapes to Trace

Hello Kitty

Tippy

Kathy

Fifi

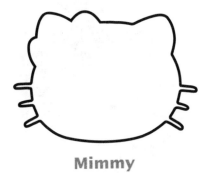

Mimmy

Hello Kitty Signs Off

I hope you enjoyed all of my favorite craft sticks projects. Tippy and I had so much fun creating and decorating them with you! Now it's time for Tippy to go home, and I'm going to curl up and take a little catnap. I'll dream up some more projects for our next Hello Kitty crafts party. See you soon!

With hugs and kisses,

xoxo Hello Kitty and Tippy